FIRST
ENGLISH
GRAMMAR

Previously published as *A Very Simple Grammar of English*.
This edition has been fully revised.

C. Blissett   K. Hallgarten

LTP
LANGUAGE

Language Teaching Publications
35 Church Road
Hove BN3 2BE

ISBN 0 906717 52 3

© Celia Blissett, Katherine Hallgarten
Language Teaching Publications 1985, 1992

Reprinted 1986, 1988, 1989, 1990, 1991
New Edition 1992
Reprinted 1994, 1996

Acknowledgements

We are grateful to Denise Chamberlain for her careful typing of a complicated
manuscript.

Cover design by Anna Macleod.

Typeset in 10pt ITC Garamond.

Printed in England by Commercial Colour Press, London E7.

Contents

Map of this book

present simple, p16, 30   present continuous, p17, 30

We **live** in Grange Road but we'**re looking** for a new flat.

past simple, p18, 31   past continuous, p19

He **rang** while I **was watching** the News.

present perfect continuous, p25   present perfect, p24, 30

I'**ve been trying** to ring her but now I'**ve written** to her.

the future, p27

I'**m going to write** tomorrow.
I'**ll write** tomorrow.
We **leave** at six tomorrow morning.
We'**re having** lunch in Oxford.

imperative, p38   if, p34

Ask her **if** she needs any help.

passive, p32

The new hospital **was opened** last year.

question word questions, p63

What happened then?
Who told you?
Where does she live?

What **can** we do about it? *p45*

I **could** come tomorrow. *p46*

I **may** come – I'm not sure yet. *p47*

Take an umbrella – it **might** rain. *p48*

I'**ll** be there but I **won't** be staying long. *p49 p49*

Would you like a cup of tea? *p50*

Shall I get a ticket for you? *p51*

They **should** be ready by Thursday. *p52*

I really **must** be going now. *p44*

You **ought to** see the doctor. *p53*

Do you **have to** book in advance? *(have) to, p54*

We'**ll have to** get some milk. *'ll have to, p55*

I'**ve got to** get to the bank this afternoon. *(have) got to, p56*

They'**ve got** three children now. *(have) got, p57*

I'**m not used to** such hot weather. *(be) used to, p58*

Have you **got used to** your glasses yet? *(get) used to, p58*

I **used to** live in Oxford. *used to, p59*

It's a lovely day, **isn't it.** *tags, p60*

5

Map of this book

p86 p98 p86

It's difficult to do anything **because it's** so late.

p98

He isn't French **although** he has a French car.

conditions, p34

If you worked harder, you could pass!
If I see her I'll tell her.

p88

Is **there** a post office near here please?

p94 prepositions of time, p92

The chemist's **in** New Street is open **from** 8am **to** 10pm.

suffixes, p103 prefixes, p103

You need to **brighten** this room – why not **re-paint** it?

p106 p106

That's not his **parents'** car –that's **Jim's** own!

The forms of the verb

In this book these terms are used:

	First Form (Infinitive)	Second Form (Past Simple)	Third Form (Past Participle)
Regular verb	ask	asked	asked
Irregular verb	give	gave	given

FIRST **FORM**	ask give	Infinitive Imperative Present Simple	I'd like to **ask** him to the party. **Ask**! Somebody might know. Children **ask** a lot of questions.
SECOND **FORM**	asked gave	Past Simple	I **asked** a policeman where it was.
THIRD **FORM**	asked given	Present Perfect Past Perfect Passive	I**'ve asked** John to bring his car. Somebody **had** already **asked** her. I**'ve been asked** to help on Saturday.
THE –S **FORM**	asks gives	Present Simple with *he, she, it*	Maria is at the age when she **asks** a lot of questions.
THE –ING **FORM**	asking giving	Verbal noun Continuous forms	**Asking** too many questions annoys people. Who **are** you **asking** to the party?

We'd like everyone to **give** something.
Give her some flowers – she'll like that.
Most people **give** presents at Christmas.

My parents **gave** it to him.

Have you **given** your name to the Secretary?
They asked us but we'**d** already **given** something.
I'**ve been given** a free ticket.

He **gives** a lot of time to other people.

Giving is better than taking.
What **are** you **giving** her for her birthday?

Full verbs and auxiliaries

English has two kinds of verbs: **full verbs** and **auxiliaries**:

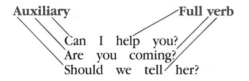

Auxiliary   Full verb

Can I help you?
Are you coming?
Should we tell her?

Full verbs

– tell you 'what happened' or 'what the situation is'
– usually have four forms: **walk walks walked walking**
– an irregular verb can have five: **go goes went gone going**

Most verbs are full verbs; sometimes they are called 'ordinary verbs', or 'main' verbs.
The patterns for main verbs are on pages 16 to 31.

Auxiliaries

There are only a few auxiliaries.
Modals: can could may might will would shall should must ought to
The modals add extra meaning. They are on pages 44 to 53.

Auxiliaries used to make structures

(be)	am	is	are	was	were	been	being
(have)	has	have	had	having			
(do)	do	does	did	done	doing		

(be) always behaves like an auxiliary. Its patterns are on page 39.
(have) is sometimes an auxiliary and sometimes a main verb. The main verb patterns are on pages 40, 41.

(be)	present continuous, page 17	They**'re looking** for a new flat. He**'s taking** his driving test tomorrow.
	past continuous, page 19	**Was** he **watching** us? Who **were** they **waiting** for?
	passive, page 32	They **are made** of pure silk. It **was built** in 1937.
	+ *going to,* page 27	I think it**'s going to** rain. **Were** you **going to** tell him?
(have)	present perfect, page 24	He**'s lost** his glasses. I**'ve** never **eaten** passion fruit before.
	past perfect, page 25	We **hadn't taken** a map, so we got lost.
	(have) got, page 57	**Have** you **got** tickets? I **hadn't got** my passport with me.

(do)	negative of a full verb
	    – present
	    – past
		I **don't understand.**
		We **didn't bring** the car after all.

	questions with a full verb – present – past	**Do** you **eat** meat? **Did** they **come** by plane?
	emphasis with a full verb – present – past	I **do like** your hair. We **did enjoy** ourselves.
	instead of repeating a full verb	I like my coffee strong. ▷ So **do** I. Jayne went but Joyce **didn't.**

Auxiliaries

These words, called the modal auxiliaries, are used *only* as auxiliaries:

can	I **can't** tell you – it's a secret.
could	Nobody **could** tell me your phone number.
may	It **may** rain later.
might	We **might** go to Spain for our holidays this year.
will	When **will** we get to London?
would	What **would** you like for your birthday?
shall	**Shall** I put the light on?
should	I think we **should** buy her a small present.
must	I **must** be going soon.

Important structures using auxiliaries:

1. Making negatives:

Add **n't** at the end of the first auxiliary; if there is no auxiliary use **(do).**

He could drive.	He **couldn't** drive.
He drives. He does drive.	He **doesn't** drive.

2. Making questions:

Change the order of the subject and the first auxiliary; if there is no auxiliary use **(do)**.

We should try to ring her.	**Should** we **try** to ring her?
He drives. He does drive.	**Does** he **drive?**

3. Making a tag:

Use the first auxiliary; if there is no auxiliary use **(do)**.

It's a lovely day.	It's a lovely day, **isn't** it.
He drives.	He drives, **doesn't** he?

4. Making a short answer:

Use the first auxiliary; if there is no auxiliary use (**do**).

Have you heard from Paul?	▷ Yes I **have.**	▷ No I **haven't.**
Will Jill be there?	▷ Yes she **will.**	▷ No she **won't.**
Do you know where it is?	▷ Yes I **do.**	▷ No I **don't.**

5. Making an interested response:

Use the first auxiliary in the answer; if there is no auxiliary use (**do**).

I've been there before.	▷ Oh, **have** you?
He was looking for you.	▷ Oh, **was** he?
She drives an old Fiat.	▷ Oh, **does** she?
We caught the early train.	▷ Oh, **did** you?

6. Emphasis, to show special emotion:

Stress the first auxiliary; if there is no auxiliary use (**do**).

I've been waiting 10 minutes.	I can come tomorrow.
→ I **have** been waiting 10 minutes.	→ I **can** come tomorrow.
I know the way.	I waited more than an hour.
→ I **do** know the way.	→ I **did** wait more than an hour.

A general rule of spoken English:

Certain patterns are **always** used exactly the same way. If a pattern uses an auxiliary, and a sentence does not have an auxiliary: use part of (**do**) – *do, does, did* – and follow the same pattern. Some books call (**do**) the "dummy auxiliary."

Short and full forms

Short forms

Normal speech *(I'm sorry)*
Informal writing (letters to friends)

Full forms

Stress in speech *(I **am** sorry)*
At the end of a sentence. *(Yes, I am.)*
In questions. *(Are you going?)*
Most writing.

The verb (be)

I'm	you're	he's
I'm not	you're not/	he isn't
	you aren't	

I am	you are	he is
I am not	you are not	he is not

The verb (have)

we've	she's	they'd
we haven't	he hadn't	she hasn't

we have	she has	they had
we have not	he had not	she has not

The verb (do)

she doesn't
they don't
we didn't

she does not
they do not
we did not

Will

I'll
I won't

I will
I will not

Would

they'd
they wouldn't

they would
they would not

The short forms:

's   can be **is**   It*'s* raining.   She*'s* waiting.
          or **has**   He*'s* remembered.   Jack*'s* taken it.

'd   can be **had**   He*'d* already gone.   Who*'d* you told?
          or **would** I*'d* like to go.   They*'d* never believe you.

In normal speech the short, unstressed, forms are used.

The stressed form adds *extra* meaning.

I'm sorry.	Normal
I **am** sorry.	Stronger, more serious apology
I've been waiting an hour.	Fact
I **have** been waiting an hour.	Slightly annoyed
She's left.	Fact
She **has** left.	Correcting what the other person says or thinks
That was nice.	Fact, a bit cool
That **was** nice.	Enthusiastic

Present simple

I you we they	walk don't walk
he she it	**walks** doesn't walk

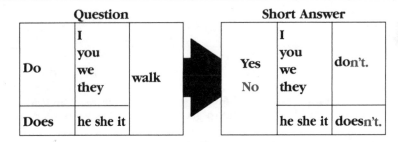

Question

Do	I you we they	walk
Does	he she it	

Short Answer

Yes No	I you we they	don't.
	he she it	doesn't.

I usually **get up** about seven.   Regular actions or events

Does Tony **drive** to work?
▷ No, he **cycles.**

The football season usually **starts** in August.

I **like** tea but I **don't like** milk in it!   Facts

What **does** this **mean** please?

The River Danube **flows** through Vienna.

Next Monday **is** a national holiday.   Facts known about the future

Classes **begin** next week.

I **don't want** to go out this evening.   Thoughts and feelings at
                                       the time of speaking
I'm sorry I **don't understand.**

I **feel** sick.

The difference between the Present simple and Present continuous (page 17) is on page 30.

Present continuous

I	'm not	
he she it	isn't 's not	coming
we you they	're not aren't	

Question		
Am	I	
Is	he she it	coming
Are	we you they	

Short Answer		
Yes No	I	am. 'm not.
	he she it	isn't.
	we you they	aren't.

're not is used more than **aren't.**

Look, Mary**'s getting** into that car.

I**'m not looking forward to** the interview.

Excuse me, **is** anyone **sitting** here, please?

Who**'s** Katy **talking** to?

At the time of speaking

They**'re building** a block of flats over there.

We**'re looking for** a new house.

Is your baby **sleeping** all night yet?
▷ No she **isn't,** not yet.

True at the moment, but not always

Karim**'s working** on night shift next week.

When **are** they **flying** to India?

Are you **coming** to the party on Saturday?
▷ No, I**'m not** as a matter of fact.

Present plans for the future

Past simple

I thought you liked spaghetti.

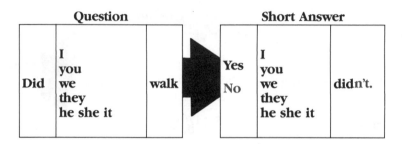

I you we they he she it	walked didn't walk

Question

Did	I you we they he she it	walk

Short Answer

Yes No	I you we they he she it	didn't.

For important verbs with different forms in the past simple – see p20 to 23.

Stefan **wanted** to catch the early train but he **missed** it.

I **told** you it **started** at 7 o'clock. I **knew** it did.

Where **did** you **go** last night?
▷ We **went** to the pub for a drink.

Did you **lock** the door?
▷ Yes, I **did,** don't worry.

Single actions, thoughts or feelings finished before the time of speaking

They **told** me I **needed** to wear glasses.

Why **didn't** you **tell** him?
▷ He **said** he **knew** about it already.

Reporting what someone said (after verbs like *said, told, asked*)

The difference between the Past simple and the Present perfect (page 24/5) is on page 31.

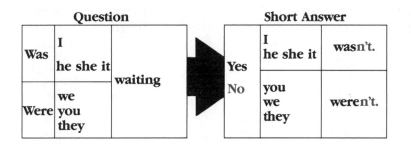

I **was watching** the News when you rang.

What **were** you **doing** when you heard the crash?
▷ I **was getting** dressed.

I **was** just **thinking** of ringing him when he walked in.

We got married while we **were living** in York.

Were they **waiting** when you got there?
▷ No, they **weren't.**

An event, finished before the moment of speaking, which went on for a period.

Often the *longer* of two actions is in the past continuous and the *shorter* in the past simple.

Irregular verbs

There are about 180 irregular verbs. Some are very unusual. Here are the most useful.

First form	Second form	Third form	First form	Second form	Third form
be	was, were	been	find	found	found
beat	beat	beaten	fly	flew	flown
become	became	become	forget	forgot	forgotten
begin	began	begun	forgive	forgave	forgiven
bend	bent	bent	freeze	froze	frozen
bite	bit	bitten			
blow	blew	blown	get	got	got
break	broke	broken	give	gave	given
bring	brought	brought	go	went	gone
build	built	built	grow	grew	grown
buy	bought	bought			
			have	had	had
catch	caught	caught	hear	heard	heard
choose	chose	chosen	hide	hid	hidden
come	came	come	hit	hit	hit
cost	cost	cost	hold	held	held
cut	cut	cut	hurt	hurt	hurt
			keep	kept	kept
do	did	done	know	knew	known
draw	drew	drawn			
drink	drank	drunk	lend	lent	lent
drive	drove	driven	leave	left	left
			let	let	let
eat	ate	eaten	light	lit	lit
			lose	lost	lost
fall	fell	fallen			
feed	fed	fed	make	made	made
feel	felt	felt	mean	meant	meant
fight	fought	fought	meet	met	met

20

First form	Second form	Third form	First form	Second form	Third form
pay	paid	paid	steal	stole	stolen
put	put	put	stick	stuck	stuck
ride	rode	ridden	take	took	taken
read	read	read	teach	taught	taught
ring	rang	rung	tear	tore	torn
run	ran	run	tell	told	told
			think	thought	thought
say	said	said	throw	threw	thrown
see	saw	seen			
sell	sold	sold	understand	understood	understood
send	sent	sent			
set	set	set	wake	woke	woken
shake	shook	shaken	wear	wore	worn
shine	shone	shone	win	won	won
shoot	shot	shot	write	wrote	written
show	showed	shown			
shrink	shrank	shrunk			
shut	shut	shut			
sing	sang	sung			
sit	sat	sat			
sleep	slept	slept			
speak	spoke	spoken			
spend	spent	spent			
split	split	split			
spoil	spoilt	spoilt			
stand	stood	stood			

Some verbs have two spellings:

burnt or **burned**
smelt or **smelled**

The verbs are:

burn   smell   learn
dream   spell   spill

Irregular verbs

Here the same verbs are in groups to make them easy to learn.

First form	Second form	Third form	First form	Second form	Third form
All forms the same			blow	blew	blown
cost	cost	cost	fly	flew	flown
cut	cut	cut	know	knew	known
hit	hit	hit	throw	threw	thrown
hurt	hurt	hurt	grow	grew	grown
let	let	let	draw	drew	drawn
put	put	put			
set	set	set			
shut	shut	shut	begin	began	begun
split	split	split	drink	drank	drunk
			ring	rang	rung
Similar sound groups			sing	sang	sung
beat	beat	beaten	shrink	shrank	shrunk
bite	bit	bitten			
eat	ate	eaten			
fall	fell	fallen	freeze	froze	frozen
forget	forgot	forgotten	speak	spoke	spoken
forgive	forgave	forgiven	steal	stole	stolen
give	gave	given	break	broke	broken
hide	hid	hidden	wake	woke	woken
shake	shook	shaken	choose	chose	chosen
take	took	taken	drive	drove	driven
tear	tore	torn	write	wrote	written
wear	wore	worn	ride	rode	ridden

First form	Second form	Third form	First form	Second form	Third form
Second and third forms the same			feed	fed	fed
bend	bent	bent	find	found	found
build	built	built	have	had	had
feel	felt	felt	hear	heard	heard
keep	kept	kept	hold	held	held
leave	left	left	make	made	made
light	lit	lit	pay	paid	paid
lend	lent	lent	read	read	read
mean	meant	meant	say	said	said
meet	met	met	sell	sold	sold
send	sent	sent	stand	stood	stood
shoot	shot	shot	understand	understood	understood
sleep	slept	slept	tell	told	told
spend	spent	spent	stick	stuck	stuck
spoil	spoilt	spoilt	win	won	won
get	got	got	shine	shone	shone
lose	lost	lost			
sit	sat	sat	**All forms different**		
			be	was/were	been
			become	became	become
			come	came	come
bring	brought	brought	do	did	done
buy	bought	bought	go	went	gone
fight	fought	fought	run	ran	run
think	thought	thought	see	saw	seen
catch	caught	caught	show	showed	shown
teach	taught	taught			

Present perfect

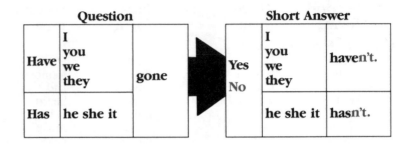

	Question					Short Answer	
I you we they	(have) 've haven't	gone	Have	I you we they	gone	Yes	I you we they	haven't.
he she it	(has) 's hasn't		Has	he she it		No	he she it	hasn't.

We haven't seen Tom for a long time.

The speaker is looking back from the present to the past.

Has Paula **taken** her driving test yet?
▷ No, she **hasn't.**

Have you ever **been** to the Tower of London?
▷ Yes, but I **haven't been** there for twenty years!

Ever is often used with present perfect to ask about before now. Note the word order: *Have you ever . . . .?*

I've never **heard** that before.

I've already **seen** him. I met him yesterday.

Often a past time adverb (*yesterday, last week*) with Past simple, but not with Present perfect.

The difference between the Present perfect and the Past simple (page 18) is on page 31.

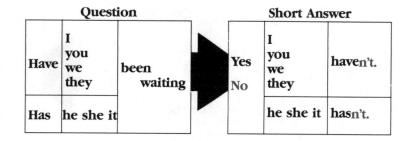

I you we they	haven't	been waiting
he she it	hasn't	

Question

Have	I you we they	been waiting
Has	he she it	

Short Answer

Yes No	I you we they	haven't.
	he she it	hasn't.

Have you **been waiting** long?

How long **have** you **been learning** English?

I**'ve been thinking** of changing my job.

Carmen **hasn't been feeling** too well recently.

Why are you crying?
▷ I**'ve been chopping** onions.

You don't look surprised.
▷ I'm not. I**'ve been expecting** this to happen.

The speaker is looking back from the present to a period in the past. The period is continuing at the moment of speaking or has stopped.

Past perfect

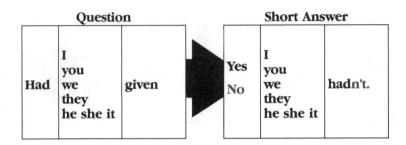

				Question				Short Answer		
I you we they he she it	'd hadn't	given	Had	I you we they he she it	given		Yes No	I you we they he she it	hadn't.

I hadn't met him until the meeting last week.

He got the job because he**'d learned** to type.

I**'d** never **seen** snow until I came to England.

We**'d finished** by twelve o'clock.

The speaker is looking back from the past on the earlier past.

There is no special verb form to talk about the future in English.

| We | 're going to leave
'll leave
're leaving
leave | at seven o'clock tomorrow morning. |

All these are correct. They give the same facts. The choice depends on the *reason* the speaker sees for the future event.

(be) going to

I'm going to give up smoking.

I	'm not	going to come
you we they	're not aren't	
he she it	's not isn't	

Question

Am	I	going to come
Are	you we they	
Is	he she it	

Short Answer

Yes	I	am. 'm not.
No	you we they	aren't.
	he she it	is

Oh dear, I**'m going to sneeze.**

Look at those clouds – it**'s going to rain.**

There is evidence (*a tickle, clouds*) now for the future event.

She**'s going to change** her job.

What **are** you **going to do** this evening?
▷ I**'m going to watch** the film on TV.

There is a long-term *decision* about the future.

The Future

'll

I won't be a moment, I'll just get my jacket.

I you we they he she it	'll won't	say

Question

Will	I you we they he she it	say

➤

Short Answer

Yes No	I you we they he she it	will. won't.

On the fast train they**'ll arrive** at 8 o'clock.

It looks as if it**'ll be** a nice weekend.

There **won't be** a Christmas party this year.

Something the speaker thinks is certain to happen.

I'm tired. I think I**'ll go** to bed.

Will Maria **be** back soon?
▷ No, she **won't be** back today, but she**'ll be** here all day tomorrow.

What **will** you do?

When **will** you **get** your results?
▷ I **won't know** before the end of August.

The speaker's opinion, or decision or feeling formed at the moment of speaking.

Is that the phone?
▷ Don't worry. I**'ll answer** it.

I**'ll** just **change** my jacket.
▷ Hurry up, or we**'ll miss** the train.

The speaker's reaction to a comment or event, formed at the moment of speaking.

Present continuous

What time **are** you **leaving** tomorrow?
▷ We**'re getting** the 6.50 train.
I**'m working** late every evening next week.
They**'re going** out this evening.

I'm playing tennis on Saturday.

The speaker *knows* because of something which has already happened, usually an arrangement with another person.

Present simple

My birthday **is** on a Wednesday this year.

Christmas Day **falls** on a Sunday this year.

Ramadan **ends** in two weeks time.

The Cup Final is on May 17th this year.

Events fixed by the calendar or an official timetable. A fact you can look up.

When you study the different future forms, the *examples* are more important than the explanations. You can't learn a rule and then use it. You will slowly build up a picture of the differences as you hear and read more natural English.

Often the differences are small, and you are not likely to be misunderstood. Be patient, and build your understanding step-by-step.

Present simple or Present continuous

If you want to understand the *difference* between these two forms, here are some more details, but remember you will build up an understanding, step-by-step, by listening to and reading natural English. Don't expect to understand the difference immediately.

The present continuous always refers to an action which the speaker sees as:

a. a *period*
b. a *limited* period

I usually *drive* to work, but I *'m walking* while the weather is so nice.

The present simple refers to an action which the speaker does **not** see as a limited period. It can be:

a. a point
b. an *unlimited* period.
c. something *always* true.
d. a general statement.

I *promise* I won't tell anyone.
Where do you *come* from?
Water *boils* at 100°C.
The journey *takes* about three hours.

Sometimes both are possible with different meanings:

I *work* in a hospital.
I *'m working* in a hospital.

I do not plan to move soon – it is my permanent job.
I expect to move soon – it is a temporary job.

Where *do* you *live?*
Where *are* you *living?*

About your *permanent* home.
To a visitor, about his or her *temporary* home.

Where *do* you *go* for your holidays?
Where *are* you *going* for your holidays?

Usually; general
This year; specific

Sometimes the objective difference is very small:

I *'m not feeling* very well.

I *don't feel* very well.

Past simple or Present perfect

Again, you will build up an understanding by listening to, and reading, English. Understanding comes step-by-step. Here are some notes to help you.

There are two different ways in English to talk about an event in the past:

The past simple suggests "then" or "at that time".
The present perfect suggests "up to now" or "before now".

I first **met** John three years ago.   The speaker looks *at* the past event from the past, in a "flash back".
I've **known** John for three years.   The speaker looks *back* at the past event *from the present,* the moment of speaking.

The facts described are the same. The speaker can use either verb form. The choice depends on the speaker's *subjective* view of the event.
The present perfect means that the past event is connected to the moment of speaking *in the speaker's mind.*

I *haven't seen* David this morning.   (but it is still morning, so I might see him)
I *didn't see* David this morning.   (the morning is over, remote)
I *haven't seen* David yet.   (yet = up to now, so *I didn't see David yet* is impossible)

Sometimes the difference is small:

Yes, I *lived* there when I was a child. (It is now remote from me)
Yes, I *'ve lived* there actually.   (You remind me NOW of something in the past)

The perfect is *not* about the action being complete or not.
It is not always about the recent past.
The only general rule is the one given above.

Passive

Present

I	'm not	
he she it	's / isn't	asked
we / you / they	're / aren't	

Question

Am	I	
Is	he she it	asked
Are	we / you / they	

Past

I / he she it	wasn't	
we / you / they	weren't	asked

Question

Was	I / he she it	asked
Were	we / you / they	

Perfect

I / you / we / they	haven't	been asked
he she it	hasn't	

Question

Have	I / you / we / they	been asked
Has	he she it	

The **Short Answers** are made in the usual way:

Were they **made** in India?   ▷ **Yes, they were.**
Have you **been offered** the job?   ▷ **No, I haven't**

The passive is used to give information in a special way (see opposite). If the person who does the action is named, *by* is the preposition. Many different tenses occur in the passive:

It **was opened** by the Queen last year.
They **had been damaged** by water.

Have you **been invited** to the wedding?
Your order **will be sent** by express delivery.

In most English sentences, the word order tells you *who* did *what*:

> A thief stole my car.

That sentence is *about* the thief; the rest of the sentence gives us *new information* about the thief.

Passive sentences are different:

> My car **was stolen**. The thief **was seen** by a policeman.

These do not tell who did what, but they are still *about* the first words (*My car*) and (*The thief*) and the rest of the sentence gives us new information.

The passive is often used:

if we don't know who did something	The parcel **was sent** over a week ago.
if no specific person did something	He **was killed** in a storm.
in general statements	Coca Cola **is drunk** all over the world.

These sentences give the same information, but are used in different situations:

Writing about Shakespeare	Shakespeare wrote Macbeth in 1606.
Writing about Macbeth	Macbeth was written in 1606.

Passive sentences are about the first words (the subject) of the sentence. The rest of the sentence gives information about the subject.

Conditions

Sometimes we talk about things which are not facts, situations which are true in certain circumstances or under certain conditions. Usually these sentences contain *if* or a similar word.

If Sara's late, she never apologises.
Sara never apologises **if** she's late.

If she worked harder, she'd pass.
She'd pass **if** she worked harder.

General conditions

Present simple		**Present simple**
Sara never apologises		she is late.
He gets angry	**if**	you argue with him.
How long does milk keep		you haven't got a fridge?

Likely conditions: things which are very likely to happen.

'll (will)		**Present simple**
The doctor'll see you		you come at nine.
I'll ask Ali	**if**	I see him.
We'll miss the bus		we don't hurry.
They won't come		the weather's bad.

Unlikely conditions: things which might happen, but probably not.

'd (would)		**Past simple**
She'd pass	**if**	she worked harder.
He wouldn't be happy		he lived on his own.

Impossible conditions

'd have + third form		Past perfect (had + third form)
I'd have told you We'd have been there on time	**if**	I had known myself. we'd caught the earlier bus.

Instructions, advice

Imperative		Present simple
Stay in bed tomorrow Get the early train	**if**	you don't feel better. you want to get there in time.

If can also join sentences with a modal auxiliary. Here are some examples:

What should I do **if** the baby cries?

Can I see the manager **if** I come back later?

May I leave **if** I finish the job before five o'clock?

You ought to go to the doctor **if** it doesn't get better soon.

If can be used with many different structures. The ones on these two pages are the most common. It is usually possible to have the *if* part of the sentence as the first or the second half of the sentence.

Unless

Conditions can also be given using *unless*:

We'll go, unless it rains.
Unless I pass, I can't go to college.

= If it doesn't rain, we'll go.
= If I don't pass, I can't go to college.

Note

The use of the sentence with *if* is the same as the sentence without *if*. The part of the sentence which begins with *if* gives details of the *special situation* the speaker is talking about.

Reported Speech

Reporting in the present tense

"The queen is arriving."
▷ Hurry up! John says she's arriving!

Present tense
Reported immediately in the same tense

Reporting *will* or *'ll*

"I'll call in on my way home."
→ He said he'd call in on his way home

'll, will, shall
→ Reported with *'d* or *would*

Reporting in the past tense

"I'm leaving tomorrow."
→ He said he was leaving tomorrow.

→ He said he was leaving the following day.

"Our cat has been run over."
→ He said that their cat had been run over."

"The weather was very good."
→ They said that the weather had been very good.

Present tense
→ Reported later the same day

→ Reported a few days later

Present perfect
→ Past perfect

Past simple
→ Past perfect

Reporting a question

"Are you ill?"
→ She asked if I was ill.

"When are you leaving?"
→ She asked when we were leaving.

"Where did you go?"
→ She asked where we had gone.

Present simple
→ Past simple with *if*

Present continuous
→ Past continuous

Past simple
→ Past perfect

Reporting with say and tell

"I don't know."

→ He said he didn't know.
→ He told me he didn't know.

"Come early."

→ He told me to come early.

The Back-shift of tenses

When reporting what someone said in the past, there are no rules which are always true. Depending on what the meaning is, different tenses are used. However, here is a useful guide:

Tense used by the speaker	Reported speech tense
Present simple	→ Past simple
Present continuous	→ Past continuous
Present perfect	→ Past perfect
Past simple	→ Past perfect
Past continuous	→ Past perfect continuous
will or *'ll*	→ *would* or *'d*

Imperative

There is no special form of the verb for the imperative in English.

Mix the flour and the sugar.   Instructions
Take two tablets every four hours.
Take the second turning on the left.

Come in, **make** yourselves at home.   Invitations
Please **start, don't wait** for me.

Open your books, **turn** to page 5 and   Telling someone what to do
look at the first picture.   (instructions or orders)
Hurry up! It's twenty past seven.
Don't forget to post that letter!
Don't be late!

Push.   Signs and notices
Insert 2 × 50p.
Keep off the grass.

Note
To suggest doing something together use *Let's*.   **Let's** go now or we'll be late.
                                                           Let's take the car.

Two negatives are possible: **Let's not** tell Jenny, she'll only worry.
                                       Don't let's tell Jenny, she'll only worry.

Present

I	'm not
you we they	're not aren't
he she it	's isn't

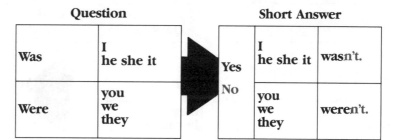

Question

Am	I
Are	you we they
Is	he she it

Short Answer

Yes	I	am. 'm not.
No	you we they	aren't.
	he she it	isn't.

Past

I he she it	wasn't
you we they	weren't

Question

Was	I he she it
Were	you we they

Short Answer

Yes	I he she it	wasn't.
No	you we they	weren't.

John **is** four now.
Omar **was** a builder in Iran.

(be) as a full verb

Are you **coming** with us?
He **was doing** 75 when the police stopped him.
Have you **been waiting** long?

(be) as an auxiliary to make continuous verb forms (see p17, 19, 25)

The bridge **was opened** by the Queen last year.
My car **has been stolen.**

(be) as an auxiliary to make passive verb forms (see p32)

39

The verb (have)

Present

I you we they	've haven't
he she it	's hasn't

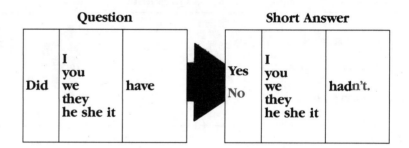

Question

Do	I you we they	have
Does	he she it	

Short Answer

	I you we they	haven't.
Yes No	he she it	hasn't.

Past

I you we they he she it	hadn't

Question

Did	I you we they he she it	have

Short Answer

Yes No	I you we they he she it	hadn't.

(have) — full verb

When (**have**) is used as a full verb it makes questions and negatives like all other full verbs.

Did you **have** a good weekend?   Pass time, experience
Have a good trip!
Are you **having** trouble with that?

What **do** you usually **have** for breakfast?   Meals, food, drink
Do you **have** lunch at work?
What shall we **have** for dinner?
Have you **had** something to drink?

I'm going to **have** a shower.   With *bath, shower*

(have) — auxiliary

When (**have**) is used as an auxiliary, use the patterns on pages 12 and 13.

Have you **brought** your bike with you?   To make perfect verb forms, see p24, 25, 26.
What a surprise! I **hadn't expected** that!

Note
(**have**) is not normally used for possession, **have got** is usually used.

(**have**) **to**   see page 54
(**have**) **got to**   see page 56
(**have**) **got**   see page 57

The verb (do)

Present

I you we they	don't	do
he she it	doesn't	

Question

Do	I you we they	do
Does	he she it	

Short Answer

Yes	I you we they	don't.
No	he she it	doesn't.

Past

I you we they he she it	didn't	do

Question

Did	I you we they he she it	do

Short Answer

Yes No	I you we they he she it	didn't.

(do) is used both as an auxiliary and as a full verb.
The full verb uses are marked in these examples.

Do you **do** your own cooking?
Who is going to **do** the washing?
Paul **did** his homework but Ann didn't **do** hers.
Did you **do** anything exciting at the weekend?

Did you **do** those letters?
▷ I'm afraid I haven't **done** them yet.

What do you **do?**
▷ I'm a nurse.

The most common use of (do) is as the 'dummy auxiliary' in English. It is used like the other auxiliaries to make questions, negatives, tags and other structures. See p12/13.

The verbs (do) and (make)

(do) and **(make)** are used in a lot of special expressions.

Usually you use **(do)** if you are thinking of an *activity*, *process* or a kind of *work*.

You use **(make)** if you are thinking of a *product* or *result*.

Expressions with (do)

Are you **doing anything special** this evening?

If you **do the washing up**, I'll **do the ironing**.

What **are** you **going to do** about it?

Have you **done your homework?**

I'll **do my best** to help you on Saturday.

If you**'re not doing anything**, could you help me?

I must **do some housework** this weekend!

He's ill, but the doctors can't **do anything** to help.

Notice these important examples:

Expressions with (make)

I've **made something special** for dinner.

I think you've **made a mistake**.

Shh . . . Don't **make** so much **noise**.

She's **made** a lot of **money**.

We'd better **make arrangements** straightaway.

Shall I **make** some **coffee?**

It's not always easy to **make friends**.

It's hard work, but we're **making progress**.

What do you do?	= What is your job?
What are you doing?	= What is your *present* activity?
What are you making?	= What will the product of your activity be?

Modal auxiliaries

1. Modals are never about facts.

2. They are about the speaker's or listener's opinion *at the moment of speaking*.

> *David has long hair* is about David. It is a fact.
> *David must get his hair cut* is about David. It is also about the *speaker's opinion*.

> Questions with a modal are about the *listener's opinion:*
> *What should I do?* (= What do *you* think is the best thing to do?)

3. They can refer to past time or future time.

I **could ride** a bike when I was five.	Past time
I **could come** tomorrow.	Future time
You **must speak** French. (I know you took lessons).	Past time
If you're going to live in France you **must speak** French.	Future time
(You'll have to learn).	

must

I must remember to post this letter.	The speaker's view of what is necessary
You **must** read this book – it's really good.	
She **mustn't** go out until she's better.	
When **must** we be there?	Asking for the listener's view of what is necessary
Must you **make** so much noise?	
I don't know her age but she **must** be over 60.	Deduction, logically necessary
You **must** be tired after such a long journey.	
This **must** be the right road.	

Can always refers to different kinds of possibility.

Can you **come** round on Friday evening? ▷ I'm afraid I **can't** manage Friday. **Can** you **tell** me the way to the Post Office, please? ▷ I'm sorry I **can't.** I'm a stranger here. **Can** you **drive?** ▷ Yes, I **can.**	Possibility
You **can't** park on a double yellow line. **Can** I leave work early today please? **Can** we bring the children with us?	Possibility decided by law or rules
Can you pass the salt please? **Can** you give me a hand with this please?	Requests (*Is it possible for you to . . . ?*)
Can I get a ticket for you? **Can** we give you a lift?	Offers (*Is it possible for me to . . . for you?*)
You **can't** be hungry. You've just had a big lunch. Anna **can't** have gone home. Her bag's still here.	Deduction – logical possibility. Always with *can't* (negative)

could

Could, like *can,* is about possibility. *Could* is more *remote* than *can;* remote relationships (polite requests), remote in time, or more remote logical possibility.

Could I speak to Hilary, please?

Could I have six of those oranges, please?

Polite requests

Gerda **could** read when she was four.

Could you get a seat on the train?
▷ I'm afraid we **couldn't.** It was very crowded.

We **couldn't** find anywhere to park.

You **couldn't** change money without your passport.

Possibility in the past

Is that Carol over there?
▷ I'm not sure – it **could** be.

Do you think Paul **could** have gone home already?

You **could** have left it on the bus.

I'm sure you **couldn't** have left it on the bus.

Take a sweater. It **could** turn cold later.

In these examples *could* is similar in meaning to *might.* Logical possibility; something *might* be true.

You **may** have dropped it in the supermarket.   Likely, but not certain. (1)

I'd take a coat – it **may** turn cold later.

I **may** not have time to phone you this evening.

Do you think it was John we saw earlier?
▷ It **may** have been, I'm not sure.

May I borrow your dictionary for a moment, please?   Asking for permission. (2)

May we have a few days to think about it?

Note
Mayn't is very unusual: *may not* is usually used.

might

I don't feel very well.
▷ It **might** be something you've eaten.

Where are you going for your holidays?
▷ I'm not sure; we **might** go to Scotland.

I'm surprised Chris isn't here yet. Do you think he **might** have forgotten?

I'm leaving early tomorrow so I **might** not see you.

Is this a 24 bus coming?
▷ It **might** be. I can't see the number yet.

Likely, but not certain.
Similar to *may* in (1) on p39.

Note
Mightn't is unusual.

will + n't = won't

Will you sign the form, please? **Will** you phone me when you arrive?	Asking someone to do something *(Will you . . .?)*
I **will** if I have time.	Agreeing
I**'ll** give you a hand with that. We**'ll** do the washing-up.	Offering to do something for someone
She **won't** tell me where she's going tonight. I **won't** work on that machine. It's dangerous. Molly's car **won't** start. The baby **won't** stop crying.	Refusing
We **won't** see you next week. We**'ll** be on holiday. I**'ll** be back in a few minutes.	Facts about the future
Wait a minute! I**'ll** just get a sweater. That's the doorbell – It**'ll** be John. I**'ll** have pizza and salad, please.	Reactions at the moment of speaking
You**'ll** catch the train if you leave now. You **won't** be happy if you don't buy it!	Likely conditions, see page 92

Note
Will not is very strong. In speech the normal form is *won't*.

would

Would you drop me at the station please?   Requests

Would you mind closing the window please?

Would you mind if I came a few minutes late?

Would you like a cup of tea?   Offers and invitations

Would you like to come with us?
▷ That's very kind of you. I'd love to.

Would you like some more cake?
▷ No thank you, I'm fine but it's very nice.

What would be the best thing to do?   Advice

What would you do?
▷ If I were you I'd see the doctor.

They wouldn't stop the noise even when I asked.   Refusing

My car wouldn't start this morning.

I don't know what was wrong with the baby, but
she wouldn't stop crying.

You wouldn't enjoy the film, I don't think.   Talking about a hypothetical situation

Shall I bring my sleeping bag?
▷ That would help.

Shall we pick you up at the station?
Shall I get a ticket for you?

Offering to do something

Shall we go for a walk after lunch?
Who **shall** we ask to the party?
What **shall** we do about it?

Suggestions

Note
Shall is unusual in modern English except in questions with *Shall I . . . ?* and *Shall we . . . ?*

should

You **should** tell the police about it.

I think you **should** go to the doctor.
▷ Perhaps I **should.**

If you don't feel better you **should** go to bed.

The train **should** be there by four o'clock.

Excuse me, I think it **should** be £2, not £3.

You **should** have told me that you don't eat meat.

Kurt **shouldn't** have left without paying.

The *speaker's* view of the correct situation, or thing to do.

Do you think I **should** tell Peter?

What do you think I **should** do?

Asking the *listener's* view of the correct thing to do.

Note
Questions with *Should I/we . . .?* are unusual; *Do you think I/we should . . . ?* is the usual form.

ought to

I you we they he she it	ought not to	take

Question forms are very unusual (see below).

I **ought to** ring my mother.

You **ought to** phone your parents.

What do you think we **ought to** do about it?

People **ought not to** park here – it's dangerous.

Obligation (usually moral)

Note

Oughtn't is unusual; the usual form is *ought not*.

Questions like *Ought we to . . . . ?* are very unusual; the usual form is *Do you think we ought to . . . ?*

(have) to

Present

I you we they	don't **have to**	ask
he she it	**has to** / doesn't **have to**	

Question

Do	I you we they	**have to**	**ask**
Does	he she it		

Short Answer

Yes	I you we they	don't.
No	he she it	doesn't.

Past

I you we they he she it	**had to** / didn't **have to**	**ask**

Question

Did	I you we they he she it	**have to**	**ask**

Short Answer

Yes No	I you we they he she it	didn't.

Children over 14 **have to** pay full price.
The doctor says he **has to** stay in bed.
Did you **have to** wait long?
You **have to** be at the airport very early
because they **have to** search all the bags.

Necessity based on:
a rule
an authority
circumstances

Note
(have) to is used for *objective* necessity; *must* for what the *speaker thinks* is necessary.

We *have to* be there by four o'clock.
We *must* be there by four o'clock.

Suggests: *They close the doors at four.*
Suggests: *I think all the seats will be taken by four.*

I'll have to get some more coffee.

We**'ll have to** paint the house before we sell it.
We**'ll have to** go or we'll miss the last bus.
It's broken – you**'ll have to** buy a new one.
I'm afraid she**'ll have to** go into hospital.

The speaker's idea of something necessary

Negatives

don't have to = it is *not necessary* that . . .

You **don't have to** buy a ticket.
We **didn't have to** wait at all.

mustn't = it is *necessary not* to . . .

I **mustn't** forget to post this letter.
You **mustn't** take more than two of these pills at a time.

Note

Don't have to and *Don't need to* are very similar in meaning:

I'm sure we *don't need to* ask.   = I'm sure we *don't have to* ask.

You *don't have to* be here before 9.   = You *don't need to* be here before 9.

(have) got to

Present

I you we they	've haven't	got to take
he she it	's hasn't	

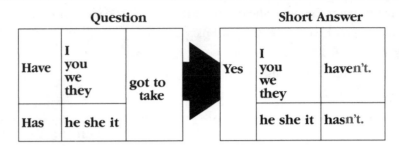

Question

Have	I you we they	got to take
Has	he she it	

Short Answer

Yes	I you we they	haven't.
	he she it	hasn't.

He's **got to** stay in bed for a few days.

You've **got to** put two 10 pence coins in to make it work.

I **haven't got to** get up early in the morning.

Sorry I can't stop – I've **got to** get to the bank before half past three.

Have we **got to** show our passports?

Note
(have) to and *(have) got to* are used with the same meaning.
had got to is unusual in the past; *had to* is normally used.

They've got two children.

(have) is not normally used to talk about possession; *(have) got* is normally used.
(have) got makes questions and negatives using *(have)* as auxiliary.
had got is unusual in the past; *had* is normally used.

Present

I you we they	've haven't	got
he she it	's hasn't	

Question

Have	I we you they	got
Has	he she it	

Short Answer

Yes	I you we they	haven't.
No	he she it	hasn't.

Past

I you we they he she it	'd hadn't	got

Question

Had	I you we they he she it	got

Short Answer

Yes	I you we they he she it	hadn't.
No		

We **haven't got** a phone.
Anna**'s got** dark hair and blue eyes.
Have you **got** change for a pound please?
▷ I'm afraid I **haven't.**
They **hadn't got** any apples so I bought
some pears instead.

Possession

Have you **got** a free evening next week?
Excuse me, **have** you **got** a minute please?
Have you **got** an appointment?

Certain expressions of time

(be) used to, (get) used to

I'm **used to** gett**ing** up early.

He**'s not used to** driv**ing** on the left.

We **aren't used to** very hot weather in England.

To talk about what is normal

How's your new job?
▷ Oh I**'m getting used to** it, thank you.

Have you **got used to** our winters yet?
▷ I**'m getting used to** them, slowly!

I **was** just **getting used to** my old job when they moved me.

I don't like this new medicine.
▷ Don't worry. I'm sure you**'ll** soon **get used to** it.

To talk about the process of changing to a new normal situation

Note
(be) used to and *(get) used to* use these patterns:

He	isn't hasn't got	used to	his new job yet. it. living in London.	(noun) (pronoun) (. . . *ing* form)

used to + first form, *I used to live in London*, has a different meaning; see page 59.

used to

I you we they he she it	used to didn't use to	live

Question forms are unusual.

I **used to** smoke.

He **used to** play squash until his accident.

Do you work full time?
▷ Not now, but I **used to** before I had the children.

It's funny. I really enjoy cricket now but I **didn't use to.**

Something which was true for a period in the past but was not true later

Note
Did you use to . . . ? is unusual; we usually say *You used to . . . , didn't you?*

Tags

It's a lovely day, isn't it.

Tags are very important in spoken English. They are not used in written English.

Say	Mean
It's a lovely day, **isn't it.**	Say something about the weather.
That was a super film, **wasn't it.**	Say something about the film.
That's a good idea, **isn't it.**	Give me your opinion about it.
Things were different then, **weren't they.**	Talk about your memory of the situation.

Tags are not questions. They usually invite the other person to make a comment.

How to make tags

Use the first auxiliary to make the tag. If there is no auxiliary use *do, does* or *did*.

Positive sentence	Negative tag	Negative sentence	Positive tag
It**'s** a beautiful day,	**isn't it.**	It **isn't** a very nice morning,	**is it.**
You**'ve** been to London,	**haven't you.**	You **haven't** been to London,	**have you.**
It **must** have been David,	**mustn't it.**	It **couldn't** have been David,	**could it.**
You **know** Mary,	**don't you.**	They **don't** eat pork,	**do they.**
She **drives** to work,	**doesn't she.**	Your mother **doesn't** speak English,	**does she.**
They **played** well,	**didn't they.**	You **didn't** leave the window open,	**did you.**

Most tags ask the other person to *comment*. If you say them like questions they ask the other person to *confirm* what you think:

Say	Mean
You don't smoke, do you?	I don't think you do – is that right?
Sheila isn't married, is she?	I don't think she is – is that right?

The sentence *you* use shows what *you* think:

Paul's been to London, hasn't he?	The speaker thinks Paul *has*.
Paul hasn't been to London, has he?	The speaker thinks Paul *hasn't*.

You don't just *answer* invitation tags, you add some extra information:

You can speak German, can't you.	▷ Yes, a bit. I learned at school.
There's a car park near the theatre, isn't there.	▷ Yes, in Gifford Street.
We haven't got time for a cup to tea, have we.	▷ No, the train goes at ten to.

Notice these:

There's a post office in Churchill Road, isn't there.

There in the tag too.

You will remember to post that letter, won't you.

The tag for *will* is *won't*.

Let's have a cup of tea, shall we?

The tag for *let's* is *shall we*.

61

Asking questions — the basic pattern

Statement	Question		
	Auxiliary	**Subject**	**Verb**
Sentences with one auxiliary			
It was raining.	Was	it	raining?
He's seen the doctor.	Has	he	seen the doctor?
You can read my writing.	Can	you	read my writing?
Sentences with more than one auxiliary — use the first			
She's been waiting a long time.	Has	she	been waiting a long time?
They're going to buy a new car.	Are	they	going to buy a new car?
Sentences with no auxiliary — present simple and past simple — use (do)			
The bus stops in Salisbury Road.	Does	the bus	stop in Salisbury Road?
She caught the plane.	Did	she	catch the plane?

Note

For **(be)** see page 39; for **(have)** see page 40.

John told Mary. **Who told Mary?**

Who did John tell?

1. The question is about the *subject* of the sentence.

2. The question is about the *object* of the sentence. The question is made in the usual way. (See **2.** below)

1. Here are some more examples with *who* or *what* as the subject:

Who paid?
Who told you?
Who lives next door?
Who brought Amin to work?

Who knows about it?
What happened?
What caused the accident?

2. Most question word questions are made in this way:

Question word	auxiliary	subject	verb
How many	did	you	buy?
How often	have	you	been there?
How	can	I	get in touch with you?
Which	did	you	choose?
When	will	she	know the results?
Where	were	they	going?
What	are	we	going to do about it?
Who	could	we	ask to help?
Why	would	you	like to go?
Which floor	do	you	live on?
Which night	are	they	going to the cinema?
Whose car	were	you	driving yesterday?
Whose book	did	you	borrow?

Expressions with the . . . ing form

All these are followed by the . . . .*ing* form of the verb.

(do) the	Have you **done the ironing?**
go	They usually **go shopping** on Saturday.
hate/love	I **hate/love getting up** early.
enjoy	Do you **enjoy playing** tennis?
finish	I'll just **finish writing** this letter.
stop	Jack's **stopped smoking** at last.
suggest	Peter **suggested going** to Ibiza.
need	My hair **needs washing**.
can't help	I **can't help wishing** I hadn't told you.
go on	He **went on complaining** all evening.
miss	Do you **miss living** in London?
Would you mind . . .	**Would you mind lending** me your pen, please?
(be) used to	**I'm not used to driving** in town.
afraid of	**I'm afraid of flying.**
without	You can't get in **without paying.**
It's worth/It's no use . . .	**It's worth/no use applying** for a grant.
It's no good. . .	**It's no good complaining**
instead of	We'll drive **instead of catching** the train.
What about . . .	**What about having** a picnic?
interested in	**I'm not interested in spending** more than £3.

Expressions with the infinitive

All these expressions are followed by the infinitive with *to* :

learn	We **learned to swim** before we started school.
hope	They **hope to finish** work early.
promise	I **promise to be** a better student.
refuse	Dick **refused to pay** the bill.
decide	Have you **decided to fly**?
mean	I'm sorry. I **meant to let** you know.
offer	Did she **offer to give** you a lift?
agree	Let's **agree to differ**!
anxious	My mother was **anxious to hear** the news.
prepared	I'm not **prepared to work** at weekends.
likely	He's **likely to arrive** late.
afraid	Liz was **afraid to go** to the police.
sorry	I was very **sorry to hear** about your accident.

Verb + object + infinitive with *to* :

ask	We had to **ask John to leave**.
tell	Please **tell your friends to come** a bit later.
persuade	Can you **persuade Bill to lower** the price?

Some verbs can be followed by the infinitive or the *-ing* form:

love   **hate**   **begin**   **try**   **prefer**   **start**

Note

I remember sending you an invitation. = in the past
Remember to send me a card.   = in the future

65

Phrasal Verbs

Many verbs in English are made of two, or sometimes three, words. Even if you know the meaning of each word, you cannot guess the meaning of the words together.

drop = *fall* or *let fall*
drop in = *visit*

Here is a list of the most common.

Phrasal verb	Example	Meaning
break down	The car **broke down** at the weekend.	stop functioning
bring up	Children are **brought up** differently in other countries.	educate in the family
call back	Could you **call back** tomorrow please?	telephone again
call for	I'll **call for** you at 7 o'clock.	collect
call off	They've **called off** the strike.	cancel
carry on	Are you going to **carry on** studying German?	continue
catch up	You set off – I'll **catch** you **up.**	hurry after and join
close down	The factory **closed down** last year.	close permanently
come from	He **comes from** Bangladesh.	was born in
drop in	Why not **drop in** on your way home from work?	visit casually
eat out	It's nice to **eat out** for a change.	eat in a restaurant
fall out	Liz and Jack **have fallen out** again.	quarrel
fall through	I'm afraid our holiday plans **have fallen through.**	collapse (plan, arrangement)
fill in	Would you **fill in** your name and address please?	complete (a form)
find out	I hope nobody **finds out.**	discover the truth

Phrasal verb	Example	Meaning
get back	We **got back** from France last night.	return
get off	You **get off** at the end of East Street.	leave the bus
get on	How **are** the children **getting on** at school?	succeed
get on with	I **get on** very well **with** him.	agree, work well together
get out of	I can't **get out of** it.	avoid
get over	I had an operation but I**'m getting over** it now.	recover
get round to	I **haven't got round to** writing to him yet.	find time to do
get through	Did you **get through?**	make a successful phone call
get up	I **got up** at 7 this morning.	rise from bed
give up	I know it's difficult, but **don't give up!**	stop trying
go off	I think the milk**'s gone off.**	become bad (of food)
grow up	Children **grow up** more quickly nowadays.	mature
hang up	She **hung up** on me!	finish a phone call
have on	You**'re having** me **on!**	tease
hold on	Can you **hold on** a moment please?	wait, particularly on the phone
keep up	How long do you think they can **keep** that **up?**	maintain, continue
knock down	She **was knocked down** in First Avenue.	be in a traffic accident
laugh at	**Are** you **laughing at** me?	be amused by
let down	You **won't let** me **down**, will you?	disappoint
lie in	I'm going to **lie in** in the morning.	stay in bed
look after	Who**'s looking after** the children?	take care of

Phrasal verb	Example	Meaning
look at	What **are** you **looking at?**	examine carefully
look for	They**'re looking for** 20 new staff.	seek
look forward to	I'm really **looking forward to** my holiday.	anticipate with pleasure
look out for	I**'ll look out for** you at the station.	try to meet
look up	You can **look** it **up** in the dictionary.	seek information in a book
pack up	It's time to **pack up** and go home.	stop
pay back	If you lend me it I'll **pay** you **back** tomorrow.	return a debt
pay off	He **was paid off** at the end of June.	make redundant
pick up	Can I **pick** you **up** at the station?	collect (by car)
put off	Shall we **put** it **off** until next week?	delay
put off	I hope I**'m** not **putting** you **off.**	distract
put on	Don't forget to **put** your coat **on.**	wear
put through	Could you **put** me **through** to Mr Wilson please?	connect, on the telephone
put up	Can I **put** you **up** for the weekend?	accommodate
put up with	I'm afraid you'll just have to **put up with** it.	tolerate
ring back	Can you **ring back** please?	re-telephone
run out of	We**'ve run out of** sugar.	(there's no . . . left)
save up	I**'m saving up** for my holiday.	put aside money
see off	Can we **see** you **off** at the airport?	go with to station, airport etc.
set off	What time shall we **set off?**	start a journey
settle down	My mother thinks I should **settle down.**	establish a regular home

Phrasal verb	Example	Meaning
show off	Stop **showing off!**	boast, look for compliments
sleep in	Sorry I'm late – I **slept in.**	wake up late
sort out	These files need **sorting out.**	arrange systematically
stand up for	You have to **stand up for** what you believe.	defend
take after	Carol **takes after** her father.	resemble
take off	Would you like to **take** your coat **off?**	remove (clothes)
take off	What time do we **take off?**	(for a plane)
tell off	I **told** the children **off.**	reprimand
think about	What **are** you **thinking about?**	consider
think of	You should have **thought of** that earlier.	pay attention to
think over	I'd like to **think** it **over** for a while.	consider carefully
try on	Could I **try** it **on** please?	check clothes (for size etc)
turn down	His application **has been turned down.**	refuse, reject
turn off	Would you **turn** the tap **off** please?	stop
turn on	Would you **turn** the television **on** please?	switch on
turn up	I can't hear it. Can you **turn** it **up** please?	make louder (radio, TV)
wake up	What time did you **wake up?**	wake from sleep
walk out	The whole work force **walked out.**	go on strike
wash up	Who's going to **wash up?**	wash dishes
wear out	These shoes **have worn out** very quickly.	become old and unuseable
wrap up	Would you like me to **wrap** it **up** for you?	put in paper

a, an

an in front of a vowel *sound*
in front of **a e i o u**   in *front of h* when it is not sounded

an	apple egg island	orange uncle		**an**	hour	honour

a in front of all other letters   in front of **u** and **eu** when it sounds like *you*

a	bag child face	girl house		**a**	university	European

She's **a** dentist.   With a singular (countable) noun
We had **an** argument.
A pound of tomatoes please.

a hundred, **a** thousand, **a** million   With certain numbers

a dozen, **a** couple of, **a** pair of, **a** lot, **a** few, **a** little   With certain quantities
We spent **a** couple of weeks in Spain.
There were **a** lot of people at the game.

30 pence **a** pound   Costs
sixty miles **an** hour   Measurements

Note
a/an is normal, *one* is used for emphasis:
      A: A coke and two lemonades, please.
      B: Two lemonades and two cokes.
      A: No, two lemonades and **one** Coke, please.

Only one spelling: **The** dress, girl, police, children

Two pronunciations: in front of a consonant sound / ðə /   **the** side
                            in front of a vowel sound   / ð i: /   **the** apple, **the** engine, **the** ice-cream,
                                                       the other one, **the** umbrella

                                                the is usually used with:

I left **the** car in George Street.   a person or thing already
(= *my* or *our* car)   identified or known

Which dress did you buy?
▷ **The** blue one.

Can you close **the** door please?

He bought the house next to **the** Post Office.

the China Sea, **the** Ganges, **the** Alps   names of seas, rivers, mountain ranges
Lake Ontario, Windermere   (but *not* lakes)

the Taj Mahal, **the** White House   important buildings
the Eiffel Tower

He plays **the** guitar and **the** piano.   musical instruments

Note

1. Most street names do **not** have *the* in front of them: George Street, Queens Road, but *the* High Street.

2. *The* is not used with **at work, at home, at school, go to work, go home, go to school:**
   He goes to school at eight o'clock. What time does he go home?

3. *The* is not used with nouns used with a general meaning: *Milk is good for you. I don't like coffee.*

Countable and uncountable nouns

English nouns are divided into two groups:

Countable nouns
Are seen by the speaker in *units*

a glass   **a cup**

a glass of water   **a cup of tea**

a spoonful of sugar   **a slice of bread**

Uncountable nouns
Are **not** seen by the speaker in *units*

water   **tea**

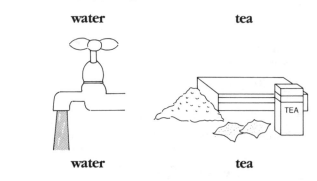

water   **tea**

sugar   **bread**

Countable nouns

– have singular and plural forms

– take singular and plural verbs

   That **boy is** French.
   Those **boys are** French.
   The **timetable changes** tomorrow.
   The **timetables** all **change** tomorrow.

– can have **a/an** and numbers in front of them

   an apple   **a** good idea
   four apples   **three** good ideas

– have **not many** in front of them

   He has**n't many** friends.
   There were**n't many** people there.

– have **a few** in front of them

   Will you have **a few** more cherries?

Uncountable nouns

– only have one form

– always take a singular verb

   Music helps me to relax.
   Their **furniture is** very modern.
   Too much **coffee isn't** good for you.
   The **weather was** beautiful all week.

– never have **a/an** or a number *directly* in front

   weather   information   advice
   furniture leather

– have **not much** in front of them

   He has**n't much** money.
   We have**n't** had **much** information yet.

– have **a little** in front of them

   Will you have **a little** more ice-cream?

Note
Much and *many* are used in *negatives* and *questions;* in positive remarks *a lot of* is normally used:

   There were **a lot of** people in town today.
   We had **a lot of** trouble getting here.

a . . . of . . .

a piece of advice

To make countable quantities with uncountable nouns use *a . . . of . . .*

a	piece pound pint jar glass tin	of	information butter milk jam water soup	a	packet bit slice litre plate tube	of	rice luck toast oil spaghetti toothpaste

Some words which are countable in some other languages are uncountable in English:

advice   information   news   luggage   knowledge   furniture   health

Some words can be used in two different ways, one countable, one uncountable:

There's *a hair* on your coat.

What *a* lovely *colour!*

Have some more *potatoes*.
▷Just *a few* please.

Her *hair* is beautiful.

Television is very dull without *colour*.

Have some more *potato*.
▷Just *a little* please.

Most nouns make their plural by adding −s.
There are three different pronunciations:

packet	packets	add /s/	after a voiceless sound (see p104)
hand	hands	add /z/	after a voiced sound (see p104)
face	faces	add /iz/	after these sounds /s/ /z/ / ʃ / / tʃ / /dʒ/

Some common plurals are different:

woman	**women**	wife	**wives**
man	**men**	knife	**knives**
child	**children**	foot	**feet**
person	**people**	tooth	**teeth**
potato	**potatoes**	baby	**babies**
bus	**buses**	lady	**ladies**
glass	**glasses**	city	**cities**
match	**matches**	sheep	**sheep**

some, any

some is about *part,* or *not all;* **any** is about *all* or *none.*

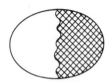

I like **some** fruit.

I like **any** fruit.

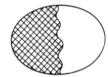

I don't like **some** fruit.

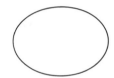

I don't like **any** fruit.

any

She doesn't drink **any** alcohol, not even beer.	None
There aren't **any** shops near our flat.	
You can take **any** bus from the station.	All
When can you come round? ▷ **Any** day next week.	
I like **any** kind of cheese.	
Did you take **any** photographs?	"Open" questions
Have you **any** small change, please?	

some

Some of the trains stop here but some don't.

Some people thought it was too expensive.

I like **some** pop music, but not all.

Not all

I've bought **some** tea but we need **some** sugar.

General quantity

Would you like us to bring **some** sandwiches with us?

I'd like **some** information about flights to Paris please.

These words are used in the same way:

somebody   **someone**   **something**   **somewhere**
anybody   **anyone**   **anything**   **anywhere**

There's **somebody** outside to see you.

We can go **anywhere** with this ticket.

There's **something** wrong with my arm.

I don't think there's **anything** we can do about it.

Let's go **somewhere** warm this year!

I've never been **anywhere** in Scotland except Glasgow.

These two questions are similar in meaning:

Can I get you **something** to eat?

Can I get you **anything** to eat?

any suggests an **open** question: *I don't know if you would like a sandwich or not.*

some suggests a **restricted** question: *You must be hungry. I suppose you are ready to eat.*

Adjectives

My wallet is **black**.
I've lost a **black** wallet.
I've lost a **black leather** wallet.

Adjectives give more information about a noun.

The boy was **late.**
The girls were **late,** too.

Singular and plural are the same.

She's a **really nice** person.
It's **very cheap.**

Use *very* or *really* to make an adjective stronger.

		Comparative	Superlative
Short adjectives			
one syllable	**cheap**	**cheaper**	**the cheapest**
two syllables ending in -y	**early**	**earlier**	**the earliest**
Long adjectives			
two syllables	**careful**	**more careful**	**the most careful**
more syllables	**difficult**	**more difficult**	**the most difficult**
Irregular adjectives			
	good	**better**	**the best**
	bad	**worse**	**the worst**

Gabi is taller than Ahmed.

Comparison of Adjectives

Ahmed is **older than** Razi.

The book is **better than** the film.

This baker is **more expensive than** the one round the corner.

Have you any **smaller** oranges?

Have you anything a bit **cheaper?**

I think yours is **better.**

Comparative + *than*

Maria is **as old as** Marco.

Gas isn't **as expensive as** electricity.

Was he **as angry as** he looked?

as + adjective + *as*

Superlatives

Razi is **the tallest** in the class.

Gabi is **the most careful** driver I know.

How much is **the cheapest** flight to Athens?

The **most expensive** isn't always **the best.**

Where's **the nearest** toilet, please?

the + superlative

Adverbs

Regular

Adjective		Adverb	
slow	careful	slowly	carefully
easy	sensible	easily	sensibly

He's a slow reader.
It's easy to make it yourself.

He reads slowly.   **+ -ly**
You can easily make it yourself.   **-y →ily**

Irregular

Adjective and adverb the same:

hard	late	early
fast	straight	
harder	earlier	faster

Adjective	Adverb
He has long **straight** hair.	Go **straight** along Cromwell Road . . . .
Let's catch the **late** train.	The train arrived 10 minutes **late.**
She's a **hard** worker.	She works **hard.**
Is there an **earlier** train?	Can you come to me **earlier** than 10, please?
The train is **faster,** but more expensive.	I wish I could read **faster.**

	Adjective	Adverb	
They're a good team.	**good**	**well**	They played well last Saturday.
These are a better buy.	**better**	**better**	Do you feel better now?

These words look like adverbs formed in the usual way but have special meanings:

nearly	= almost	Be careful! You **nearly** spilt your tea.
hardly (any)	= almost none	There's **hardly** any butter left.
lately	= in the near past	I haven't seen her **lately.**
shortly	= in the near future	I'll have to be going home **shortly.**
directly	= immediately	I'll let you know **directly** I hear myself.

Making adverbs stronger

carefully   **more carefully**   **much more carefully**   **as carefully as possible**

You must do your homework **carefully.**   → You'll have to do it again **much more carefully.**
Please tell him **soon.**   → Please tell him **as soon as possible.**

Comparing adjectives or adverbs

The same structures are used for comparing adjectives or adverbs:

Comparative + than   Ahmed is **older than** Razi.
    This restaurant is **more expensive than** that one.

    She speaks English **more confidently than** her brother.
    Liverpool played **better than** they did last week.

Not as . . . as   Razi is**n't as old as** Ahmed.
    Chinese food is**n't as interesting as** Indian.

    He does**n't** speak English **as confidently as** his sister.
    Liverpool did**n't** play **as well as** they did last week.

Position of adverbs

The rules are very complicated. Here are some useful tips:

1. If you are unsure, put the adverb *at the end* of the sentence.

2. These adverbs of time usually come after (**be**) or after the first auxiliary.

always, often,	Peter is **never** late.
usually, sometimes,	You must **always** lock the door.
never, already	We've **sometimes** had lunch at work.

3. These adverbs make an adjective or adverb stronger or weaker.
They come *in front of* the adjective or adverb.

very, too, so,	Richard can swim **very well**.
rather, really, quite,	It's **too far** to walk.
extremely, slightly	It was **quite cold** in the water.
	This is a bad line – it's **extremely difficult** to hear you.

4. ever   mainly in questions with   Have you **ever** been to Manchester?
the present perfect

5. enough   *after* an adjective   He isn't **strong enough**.
or adverb   He didn't work **hard enough**.
in front of a noun   I haven't **enough money**.

Subject pronoun	Object pronoun	Possessive adjective	Possessive pronoun	Reflexive pronoun
I	me	my	mine	myself
you	you	your	yours	yourself
we	us	our	ours	ourselves
they	them	their	theirs	themselves
he	him	his	his	himself
she	her	her	hers	herself
it	it	its	its	itself

Use a pronoun instead of a noun when it is clear *who* or *what* you are talking about.

Object pronouns

Would you like to come with **us?**

Do you live near **them?**

Could you send them direct to **me**, please?

after a preposition

Who broke that window?
▷ It wasn't **me**.

after **(be)** instead of a subject pronoun

Can Eva send them to **me,** please?

Tony made it for **her.**

After *to* and *for* with *make, give, send, lend, pass, take, show*

Note

Yourself is for one person; *yourselves* is for more than one person.

Possessives

Adjective

Tells you who owns something

My feet hurt!
Is this **your** sweater?
I don't think this is **his** car, is it?
Sheila's left **her** bag somewhere in here.
Our children like **their** school.
What's **your** phone number?

Pronoun

Instead of a possessive adjective and a noun

▷ So do **mine!** = *So do my feet*
▷ Yes, where's **yours?**
▷ No, **his** is over there.
▷ I think this is **hers,** isn't it?
▷ Yes, **ours** like **theirs**, too.
▷ 7·′26981. What's **yours?**

Reflexive pronouns

He's cut **himself.**

Oh dear! Have you hurt **yourself?**

The subject and the object are the same.

Did you do the decorations **yourself?**
▷ I did the painting **myself,** but that's all.

Can I give you a hand?
▷ No, it's all right thanks. I can do it **myself.**

Used for emphasis

Some special expressions

Help		I live **by myself.**	= I live *on my own.*
Enjoy	**yourself!**	He lives **by himself.**	= He lives *on his own.*
Behave	**yourselves!**	They live **by themselves.**	= They live *on their own.*

84

They is used to talk about:

      1. more than one person: *The children are excited – they're going on a trip tomorrow.*

      2. a general group of people:

They are repairing the road.	*they* = the Town Council
They want to increase income tax.	*they* = the Government
They say it's a marvellous film.	*they* = a lot of people
They tell me you are changing your job.	*they* = somebody or some people

They and **their** are also used to talk about *one* person with:

some- any- no- every-	-body -one

Someone has left **their** pen on the desk.

Somebody told you, didn't **they!**

Anybody knows that, don't **they!**

Everyone has to bring **their** own food.

If **anyone** rings while I'm out, please ask **them** to ring back.

it

it is used as a pronoun in the usual way: *There is a car park but it's full at the moment.*

it is also used for:

Weather	**It's** raining. **It's** rather cold.	**It** was snowing. **It** was a very warm evening.
Time	**It's** three o'clock. **It's** getting late. **It's** a long time ago.	**It's** the fifth today, isn't it. **It's** time to go. **It's** Saturday tomorrow.
Distance	**It's** about two miles. How far is **it** to Oxford?	**It's** not far. **It's** rather a long way.

It is also used as a dummy subject when *is ('s)* is followed by certain adjectives:

It's essential to be there by 7 o'clock.

It's possible to get a bus.

It's lovely to have a day off.

It's best to get a taxi.

It's difficult to believe that.

It's interesting to see new places.

It's not true that he's changing his job.

It's better to phone her.

Note

It's no use ask**ing** Peter – he wasn't there.

It's worth ask**ing** him – he might know.

Do you prefer the blue one or the red one?

That train is too early. What time is the next (train) **one.**
The French apples are 50p, but the English (apples) **ones** are only 45p.

Use *one* or *ones* instead of repeating the same noun.

the this/that	one
which	one?

the these/those	ones
which	ones?

I'm going to make a cup of coffee. Would you like **one?**
▷ Mm yes, I'd love **one,** thank you.

Which is your bike?
▷ **The** blue **one, the one** next to the car.

Shall I use these tea-bags?
▷ No, use **the ones** on the shelf, please.

Which one do you prefer?
▷ **That one's** lovely, but I think **this one** will suit me better.

there + (be)

There	's isn't	a problem
	aren't	six

Question

Is	there	a toilet
Are		any seats

Short Answer

Yes No	there	isn't. aren't.

There's a cinema in the centre.

Is there a telephone box in the station?

There are some people waiting outside.

Are there 2 m's in 'recommend'?

There's nothing we can do about it.

There's somebody waiting for you outside.

Is there anywhere to eat near here?

When you talk about something for the first time

There must be a mistake.

There might be a strike.

There can be a lot of rain at this time of year.

There should be a bus in five minutes.

There'll be trouble when he finds out!

With an auxiliary and *be*

There isn't enough room, **is there?**
▷ Oh yes, I think **there is.**

There is repeated in the tag and in the short answer.

this	these
→o	—→ 88 ○○○
that	**those**
—→ o	—→ 88 ○○○

Use:
1. in front of a noun
2. alone when it is clear what you are talking about

Does **this** bus go to Victoria, please?
Does **this** go to Victoria please?

These strawberries are delicious.
These are delicious.

Things that are physically near.

This is the life!

These science fiction films are a waste of money.

Things which are "psychologically near"; the speaker feels they are near at the moment of speaking.

How much is **that** dress please?
How much is **that** please?

A pound of **those** tomatoes please.
A pound of **those** please.

Things which are physically remote.

That was lucky! I didn't expect **that.**

That kind of person really annoys me.

Is **that** all?

Things which are "psychologically remote" from the speaker at the moment of speaking.

that, who, which

The car that was parked outside has gone.

that, who and **which** introduce more information about a person, thing, or idea.

The woman **that** lives next door is very friendly. Tells us *which woman.*
Could I speak to the doctor **that** I saw yesterday, please? Tells us *which doctor.*
The essay **that** won the prize was written by a German student. Tells us *which essay.*

The person **who** told me had been there himself.

It was the blue car **which** caused the accident.

The thing **that** really surprised me was the price. Often used with *the thing that . . .*

The thing **that** I really enjoyed was the music.

That is usual in spoken English.

In written English use: *who* with people *which* with things.

that, who, which are usually left out if they are the object of the verb that follows.

The man **who** I saw yesterday told me to come at ten o'clock.
→ **The man I saw yesterday told me to come at ten o'clock.**

Can I collect the coat **that** I brought in last week, please?
→ **Can I collect the coat I brought in last week, please?**

about	the subject of a conversation idea, book, etc.	Tell me **about** your family. What are you thinking **about?**
at	certain special expressions	**At** home, **at** school, **at** work, **at** university, **at** the cinema, **at** the end of . . . .
by	the person or thing that did something	It was written **by** William Golding. I was shocked **by** what she told me.
	transport	We went **by** train.
for	purpose + noun or . . . *ing* form	Let's go **for** a cup of coffee. This machine's **for** peeling potatoes.
	a general period of time	We were there **for** three weeks. I haven't seen you **for** ages.
from	place of origin	Where is he **from?** They come **from** Sri Lanka.
with	in company	Would you like to come **with** us?
	what you use to do something	He cut himself **with** his pen-knife.

Prepositions — Time

On			At	
Friday	Day		**two o'clock**	Time
Wednesday morning	Day + *morning, afternoon,*		**Christmas**	Festival
Wednesday night	*evening, night*		**lunchtime**	Mealtimes
the sixteenth of March	Date		**the weekend**	
Christmas Day	Special Day		**night**	

In	
Spring	Season
1947	Year
August	Month
the morning	
the evening	

Sometimes *during* and *in* have the same meaning: *in the night* is very unusual; *during the night* is normal.

Periods

For three weeks	General period
In three weeks	Period starting from now
Three weeks ago	Period ending now

Note
ago goes *after* the period.

Sometimes we talk about a *point*
a *period* between two points

at 2 o'clock

We arrived **at** 2 o'clock.

before 2 o'clock

The doctor can't see you **before** 2 o'clock.

until 2 o'clock = not before 2

I won't be there **until** 2 o'clock.

since 2 o'clock

I haven't seen her **since** 2 o'clock.

(looking back to a point in the past,
with a perfect form of the verb.)

about 2 o'clock

We'll be there **about** 2 o'clock.

after 2 o'clock

I'll be in my office **after** 2 o'clock.

by 2 o'clock = *any* point *before* or *at* 2

or

Will we be there **by** 2 o'clock?

from 2 o'clock

They are open **from** 2 o'clock.

Prepositions — Where?

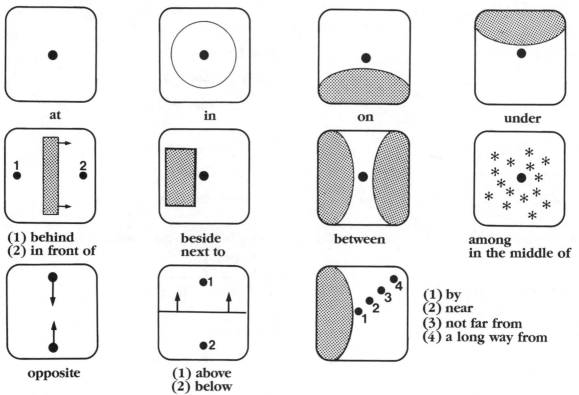

at

in

on

under

(1) behind
(2) in front of

beside
next to

between

among
in the middle of

opposite

(1) above
(2) below

(1) by
(2) near
(3) not far from
(4) a long way from

Note
To talk about a building: *David's inside. He's gone inside.*

at	He lives **at** number five. Turn left **at** the top of the stairs. I'll meet you **at** the station.	at an exact place
in	We live **in** England. Kyoko works **in** Birmingham. He lives **in** Baker Street. Were you **in** the pub last night? Throw it **in** the wastepaper bin!	a country a town a street a building or area a container
on	I'll meet you **on** the platform. There's some coffee **on** the shelf.	

under	She hid the letter **under** her book.
in front of	I'll see you **in front of** the Town Hall.
behind	Grace Road is **behind** the bus station.
next to	We live **next to** the post office.
beside	Can I sit **beside** you?
between	We live **between** Queen's Road and the sea.
in the middle of	The bus station is **in the middle of** town.
among	I found this scarf **among** some old clothes.
opposite	There's a bus stop directly **opposite** the entrance.
above	Our flat is **above** the bakers.
below	The bakers is **below** our flat.
by	I'll be standing **by** the ticket office.
near	Is there a bank **near** the station?
not far from	I walk to college because it's **not far from** home.
a long way from	We live **a long way from** the shops.

Prepositions — Where to?

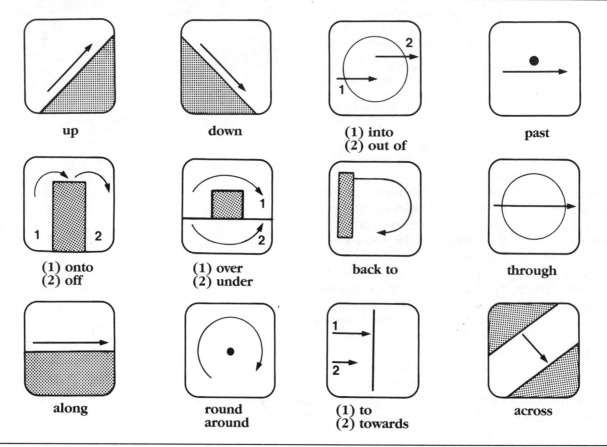

up

down

(1) into
(2) out of

past

(1) onto
(2) off

(1) over
(2) under

back to

through

along

round
around

(1) to
(2) towards

across

up	Go **up** this road then turn left.
down	Karen fell **down** the stairs.
into	I saw him getting **into** a taxi.
out of	Can you get the eggs **out of** the fridge, please.
past	He walked straight **past** me without speaking.
onto	The cat jumped **onto** her knee.
off	It fell **off** the table and broke.
round	I'm tired – I've walked **round** town today.
back to	Can we go **back to** the theatre please – I've forgotten my coat.
through	I hate driving **through** the town at this time of day.
along	They walked **along** the beach.
over	I tripped **over** a stone on the pavement.
under	The cat ran **under** the car.
to	They rushed **to** the door.
across	He ran **across** the road.

Conjunctions

A conjunction joins two ideas:

A:	Tea **or** coffee?	**or**	joins alternatives
B:	Tea, please.		
A:	Sugar **and** milk?	**and**	joins two *similar* ideas
B:	Milk **but** no sugar, thank you.	**but**	joins two *different* or *opposite* ideas

or, and, but **1.** come between the ideas they join.
2. can join two sentences.

You can change it.
You can have your money back. →You can change it **or** you can have your money back.

The surgery opens at 9.00
The surgery closes at 12.00 → The surgery opens at 9.00 **and** closes at 12.00

I'd love to come.
I'm busy on Saturday. → I'd love to come **but** I'm busy on Saturday.

so gives the *result* of the first part of the sentence. It is the second part of the sentence.

The class was boring, **so** I left.   The rent is too high, **so** we are moving.

so that gives the *purpose* for something. It is usually the second part of the sentence.

I need a nursery place **so that** I can go to work.

You'd better write it down **so that** you don't forget.

Some Expressions of Time

Past	Now
A long time ago	**In the morning**
Six or seven years ago	**Tomorrow morning**
A few years ago	**Tomorrow**
A couple of years ago	**The day after tomorrow**
Eighteen months ago	**In a day or two**
Last year	**In a couple of days**
A few months/weeks ago	**Next Saturday**
Recently	**Next Sunday evening**
The other week	**In a few days time**
Last week	**Soon**
A few days ago	**Next week**
The other day	**A week on Thursday**
The day before yesterday	**Next month**
Yesterday	**In a few weeks time**
Yesterday evening	**Next year**
Last night	**In a couple of years**
Now	**Future**

With these words the two parts of the sentence can come in either order with the same meaning:

> **Because** we were late, we took a taxi. **If** she comes, I'll tell her.
> We took a taxi **because** we were late. I'll tell her, **if** she comes.

if gives the *condition* for the other part of the sentence to be true.

> I'll do it **if** you'll help me.
> She's going to change her job **if** she can.
> **If** anyone rings, can you ask them to call back, please?

although *contrasts* two ideas.

> **Although** he's got good qualifications, he can't get a job.
> I'm going to get one, **although** they are very expensive.

because gives the *reason* for something; answers the question *Why?*

> **Because** we were late, we took a taxi.
> I didn't come **because** it was raining.

These words show the *connection in time*; answer the question *When?*

as	The lorry hit us **as** we were turning the corner.
when	I'll tell her **when** I see her.
while	They arrived **while** we were trying to phone them!
since	Where have you been living **since** you came to England?
till/until	Could you keep an eye on things **until** I get back, please?
before	I hope he gets here **before** the train leaves.
after	I'll see you here **after** I've been to the bank.
as soon as	Phone us **as soon as** your plane gets in.

1	one	first		30	thirty	thirtieth	
2	two	second		40	forty	fortieth	
3	three	third		50	fifty	fiftieth	
4	four	fourth		60	sixty	sixtieth	
5	five	fifth		70	seventy	seventieth	
6	six	sixth		80	eighty	eightieth	
7	seven	seventh		90	ninety	ninetieth	
8	eight	eighth		100	a hundred	hundreth	
9	nine	ninth		200	two hundred	two hundredth	
10	ten	tenth		1000	a thousand	thousandth	
11	eleven	eleventh		1,000,000	a million	millionth	
12	twelve	twelfth					
13	thirteen	thirteenth					
14	fourteen	fourteenth					
15	fifteen	fifteenth					
16	sixteen	sixteenth					
17	seventeen	seventeenth					
18	eighteen	eighteenth					
19	nineteen	nineteenth					
20	twenty	twentieth					
21	twenty-one	twenty-first					
22	twenty-two	twenty-second					

Write	Say		Say	Write
$\frac{1}{2}$	a half		point five	.5
$\frac{1}{4}$	a quarter		point two five	.25
$\frac{3}{4}$	three quarters		point seven five	.75
$1\frac{1}{2}$	one and a half			
$\frac{1}{6}$	one sixth			
			three point two	3.2

Have you the time, please?

What time is it, please?
▷ **It's twenty-five to seven.**

It's	exactly just about nearly	three o'clock.

What time does it start?

What time does the York train leave, please?

The train leaves at six forty-seven.

There's a train at fifteen forty.

I'll see you about sixish.
-ish gives an approximate time.

Days	Seasons	Months	
Monday	Spring	January	July
Tuesday	Summer	February	August
Wednesday	Autumn	March	September
Thursday	Winter	April	October
Friday		May	November
Saturday		June	December
Sunday			

Write: **Say:**
15th July   the fifteenth of July
21.4.54   the twenty-first of April, nineteen fifty-four.

At the beginning of a word

un-	the opposite of	*unmarried*
non-	not	*non-smoker*
anti-	against	*anti-American*
pro-	in favour of	*pro-American*
pre-	before	*pre-war*
post-	after	*post-1960*
ex-	former	*ex-President*
re-	do again	*re-start*
mis-	wrongly	*mis-understand*
over-	too much	*over-confident*

At the end of a word

-ness	adjective → noun	*darkness*
-able	verb → adjective	*washable*
-en	adjective → verb	*brighten*
-less	without	*homeless*
-ful	a quantity	*cupful*
-ish	approximately	*youngish*

Some pronunciation rules

There are two kinds of consonant sound in English:

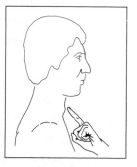

Voiced
You can feel vibration

Voiceless
You can feel no vibration

All vowel sounds are voiced.

These are pairs:

Voiced sounds:	/b/ bin	/v/ view	/ ð / with	/d/ said	/z/ zoo	/ ʒ / television	/dʒ/ bridge	/g/ go
Voiceless sounds:	/p/ pin	/f/ few	/ θ / think	/t/ set	/s/ say	/ ʃ / fish	/ tʃ / church	/k/ come

These are voiced:	/m/ men	/n/ now	/ ŋ / sing	/l/ long	/r/ red

There are three other sounds: /h/, house; /j/ yellow; /w/ wear, but these never come at the end of words.

Past simple (second form)

The past simple is usually made by adding **-ed.**
There are three pronunciations:

/t/	after a voiceless sound:	*walked*
/d/	after a voiced sound:	*opened*
/id/	after a /t/ or /d/ sound:	*waited*

Third person -s

The third person present simple is made by adding **-s.**
There are three pronunciations:

1. /s/ after a voiceless sound (except those in 3)   *waits*
2. /z/ after a voiced sound (except those in 3)   *opens*
3. /iz/after these sounds /s/, /z/, / ʃ /, / tʃ /, /dʒ /   *passes, loses, washes, watches, judges*

Plurals

Plurals are usually made by adding **-s.**
Use the same pronunciation rules as for third person-**s.**

1. voiceless: /s/   *books, cups*
2. voiced: /z/   *games, boys*
3. special sounds: /iz/   *buses, houses, wishes, watches, wages*

Some writing rules

Possession ('s or s')

's   singular

Ravi's car is a Ford.

Whose bag is that?
▷ It's **Jean's.**

's   irreglar plural nouns

The **children's** room is on the left.

s'   regular plural nouns

The **boys'** room is at the top of the stairs.

The **students'** work wasn't very good.

Spelling

-ch -sh **-x -s -o**	add **e**	before **-s**	watch	→	wat**ches**
			box	→	box**es**
			tomato	→	tomat**oes**
-e	~~e~~	before **-ed**	like	→	lik**ed**
		-es	bake	→	bak**es**
		-est	late	→	lat**est**
-y	y→ie	before **-s**	fly	→	fl**ies**
	y→i	before **-ed**	try	→	tr**ied**
		-er	easy	→	eas**ier**
		-est	lazy	→	laz**iest**
		-ly	happy	→	happ**ily**
Short vowel **+ consonant**	**double** **letter**	before **-er**	begin	→	begin**ner**
		-est	big	→	big**gest**
		-ing	stop	→	stop**ping**
		-ed	permit	→	permit**ted**

Advising

I'd complain **if I were you.**
You ought to take a couple of days off.

ought to suggests a stronger, more objective opinion.

Agreeing

I'm looking forward to the weekend.
▷ **So am I.**

Repeat the same auxiliary in the answer

I love chocolate.
▷**So do I.**

No auxiliary, use **(do)** in the answer

I don't like football on television.
▷ **Neither do I.**

Use *neither* to agree with a negative remark

Apologising

I'm sorry.
▷ **I'm sorry.**

Not really anyone's fault
– *both* say the same

I AM sorry.
▷ That's quite all right.

Stress on **am** – a real apology

Excuse me, could you change a pound please?

Excuse me before you disturb a stranger

Excuse me, please.

You want to pass someone

Have you got the tickets yet?
▷ **I'm afraid not.**

Use *I'm afraid* to 'soften' a negative or unhelpful answer

Could I speak to John please?
▷ **I'm afraid** he's out at the moment.

Basic Functions

Asking for something

A pound of apples, **please.**
Could you pass the salt, **please.**

These sound unfriendly without *please*

Asking someone to do something

Could you spell it, **please.**
Will you ask him to ring me, **please.**

Always *please* at the end

Would you mind opening the door, **please.**

Would you mind . . . ing for people you don't know

Asking for permission

May I borrow your pen?

Personal

Do you mind if I smoke?
▷ I'd rather you didn't.

Is it all right if I park here?
▷ No, I'm afraid parking isn't allowed.

More objective

Complaining

I **HAVE** been waiting twenty minutes.
It **WAS** only yesterday I bought it.
You **DID** promise to help me.

Stress the auxiliary to show you are annoyed

Correcting

I think you've made a mistake.
I think it should be £2.80, not £3.80.

Usually with *I think*

I think it was 1982, **wasn't it**?
I think the train goes at ten past, **doesn't it.**

Often with a tag (see page 60)

108

Basic Functions

Inviting

Would you like to have lunch with us?
▷ Oh thank you. I'd love to.
  That's very kind of you, but I'm afraid I can't.

Offering

Would you like a cake?   Offering something
▷ Thank you. I'd love one.

Let me carry that for you.   Offering help
We'll do the washing up.
Shall we pick you up at the station?

Can I give you a hand?   General offer to help
▷ Thank you. That's very kind of you.
  It's all right thank you. I can manage.

Have a cake!   Use the first form of the verb
Help yourself.

Refusing to do something

I **won't** work on that machine. It's dangerous.
He **won't** tell me.

Suggesting

Why don't you get a taxi?   To the other person
You could send it air mail.

Let's go now or we'll be late.   Doing something *together*
Let's go on Saturday evening.
Why don't we buy her a pen?

Useful phrases

Checking English
Could you say that again, please?
What does this mean, please?
I don't understand this.
How do you spell . . . ?
How do you pronounce this, please?
Is this correct, please?

Directions in the street
Excuse me, could you tell me where . . . is, please?
Excuse me, is there a . . . near here, please?
Turn left/right.
Take the (second) turning on the left/right.
It's on the left/right.
It's straight ahead.
Go straight along/down/up here.
It's on the corner of Brook Street and Park Lane.

Asking the time
Have you the time please?
What time do you make it, please?

When someone is going away
Have a good holiday.
Have a good trip.
Have a safe journey.

Introducing yourself
I don't think we've met before. I'm *(David Jones)*.

On the phone
May I speak to . . . please?
▷ Speaking.
Just a moment, please.
Can I take a message?
I'll ask him/her to ring you.
Sorry. I've got the wrong number.

Sending a greeting to someone
Give my regards to . . .
Remember me to . . .

On someone's birthday
Many happy returns.
Happy birthday.

On (or just after) January 1st.
Happy New Year.
▷ Thank you. The same to you.

Someone has passed an exam, got a job, won something
Congratulations!

When someone gets engaged
Congratulations. I hope you'll be very happy.

Index